FOOLS AND ANGELS

FOOLS
AND ANGELS

TESSA RANSFORD

THE RAMSAY HEAD PRESS EDINBURGH

First published in 1983 by
The Ramsay Head Press
36 North Castle Street
Edinburgh EH2 3BN

Printed in Scotland by
W. M. Bett Ltd, Tillicoultry

ISBN 0 902859 82 X

Published with the financial
support of the Scottish Arts Council

ACKNOWLEDGEMENTS

A number of poems contained in this volume
originally appeared in various periodicals including *Akros,
Chapman, Graffiti, Lines Review, New Edinburgh Review,
Poetry Review* (Leuven).

Contents

A DEEP AND DAZZLING DARKNESS

FOR POETS OF THE FIRST
SCHOOL OF POETS, 1981

Mutilated, mangled, lacerated,
My composition had been broken up.
The kind of execution perpetrated
On Cicero by that Caesarian pup.

Axe my gesturing hands, my very arms!
Van Gogh sliced off his ear, and I am less
Than he . . . Our life-work in pieces, what harms
Us further? Love has nothing to confess.

Now unexpectedly the Muse has sent
Me comforters, and several:
Poets, whose craftsmanship and wise intent
Restore my form and my material.

Sappho had never *Roy*alties like these:
Two *Robins, Jenny, John, Rose, Anne, Elise.*

this is not a half~moon bridge, for even when we can not see it to perfection a full moon is made by its reflection in Japan

THE NATURE OF REALITY

Design by Ian Appleton

INCH-SPACE OF THE HEART
A Sonnet-Sequence

We lock infinity into a square-foot of silk:
pour a deluge from the inch-space of the heart.

BASHO

PROLOGUE: EXTRAVAGANZA

While others may outskill us far in prose
In lives of duty, virtue, common-sense,
We each day labour, ready at the close
To scrap all for some lack of excellence.

A life, a year, or manuscript rejected,
Offered to others, critics and the test
Of time; which self will prove the one selected?
How many sacrificed to keep the best?

Your volte-face revolts me: Can I reverse
The poem once made? Recite it upside down?
Compose the very pieces you disperse?
Recant, or sing it to another tune?

You are the words I write, extravaganza,
My couplet, testament, my every stanza.

DISPELLS

We try to make a poem of our lives,
Choose form and metre, lovely some refrain;
With vision, brave ideas, new perspectives
We write a word or two, begin again.

It may not be a pornographic novel
Or dissertation based on careful study
Which brings rewards, respect; no interval
Shut-in-the-dark, lonely, broken, broody.

Together we composed a tragedy,
No full-scale operatic melodrama
But straight-forward, simple, saddest beauty —
The Magic-Apple-Tree of Samuel Palmer:

That poem we made I break in brutal fragments
And scatter them, dispells and disenchantments.

I

LOVE GAINSAID

What we write is easily deleted
Crossed, blotted out; for now we see
It makes no sense: This tragedy
Misunderstood by fools, was not completed.
Heretic to Plato's real ideas
You swallowed your own words, destroying them
As thoroughly as you concocted them —
Those vows, bestowals, poems, letters, tears.

How can I, unaided, keep our treasure
Heavy behind locked lips in strongroom heart,
If you decide it was but dross and lead?
There is no thought nor whisper than can measure —
No song, no symphony, nor any art —
The destitution of a love gainsaid.

THE CANVAS

With a penknife you are hacking me out
Of your heart . . . deliberately doing it.
The canvas is vandalised scratch by scrape.
It hangs there and cannot protest or shout.
I was the design for all you painted
Upon your confused, interior landscape.

Through Kafka-grey obdurate fortresses
Of colour, Pavesi trailed dejection
With yellow-ochre streaks. Subtle texture
Of Virgil or Sappho's polished verses
Dotted into fugue or variation.
I was shaped like spaces in the picture.

Is it bleak now, blanched of memory?
Have you masked the gashes there — of me?

LOVE'S BAPTISM

Let me be baptised into more pain
Or left in depths of Jordan without air
Until, immersed in ceaseless streams of care,
This body of my death be sloughed and slain.

If love be Love it cannot drown in woe
Nor burn in fire, nor cease through suffering:
This silence faintly I am entering
Is torture loathingly I undergo.

Lest I betray my own heart's certain love,
Lest I speak or scream or merely weep,
Let there be no lessening of pain.
The generosity for which we strove,
The pure ideals we longed to know and keep,
These now alone I safe-guard and maintain.

ALCHEMICAL SONNET

As that fanatical bird-singing morn
To elixir of enchantment responded,
Amazed in half-light of uncertain dawn
We lay in crazy alchemy enbonded.

The nugget of our hard-won self had melted,
A softening-unto-death and yet sublime,
But a more precious metal still unsmelted
Demanded mettle unimpaired by time.

Our hay-day soon descended into night,
Buried the fond treasure of our promise,
Unpractised our impracticable rite
Leaving ashen memories for solace.

Such ores refined in pain may lastly prove
Gold — in the alembic of our love.

GRACED WITH LIGHT

My sleep had been like sunlight filtered through
A canopy of leaves. Yet I was blind
And groped in darkness for the one I drew
Beside me: dreading to awake and find
Myself within my ownmost self confined:
No light, no tree, no lover, even sleep
Itself perhaps the making of a mind
Wandered and too overwrought to weep.

'He slumbers not who doth me ever keep'
But comes to touch and wake me with the note
Of blackbird off'ring faintly out of deep
Night — quavers of another dawn afloat.

I turn to trace dear features in outline
Graced with light and bending over mine.

THE COST

If distances were not so far
between my love and my desire,
if he were ever by my side
and nothing we need fear or hide,
if I were free, and he unbound
from his own nature's holy ground, —
how should we know the speed or strength
or height or depth or life or length
of love between us? Love so rare
that when I think on it I dare
not speak it, lest by utterance
I put to flight its innocence,
but catch my breath and silently
afford more love incessantly.

BATTLEFIELD

My poem was an epic concerning
A crusade, campaign:
Reverses, panic, slow returning
To the battle-front again.

Forced into cunning like Odysseus,
Foes behind the lines,
Friendly metaphors turning treacherous,
Foxes in the vines.

Truce was called; battle-standards lowered,
Lip-service paid to peace;
But my heroic poem was dishonoured
In its high-seriousness.

The Troy we fought for vanished in the plain:
What can we write, who won our war in vain?

SHELL-SHOCKED

I was shell-shocked and invalided out . . .
'But you can write!' they say.
'Why, everything's just fine — or just about.
Why can't you smile today?'

Can I rejoice to see the land laid waste,
Cottage and castle blackened-out with fire,
Hillside and valley cruelly defaced
With trenches and barbed-wire?

Can I smile except for this one moment
In greeting to a friend
When there is no future, and no present,
Nothing without end?

Could I divine a poem in my shock
It would be water wrenched from desert rock.

PUNCTUATION

It is not my eyes you think you're seeing
Rather full stops, black dots to mark a space,
A barrenness through moisture lost in crying,
A dark-night-of-the soul, a desert place.

It is not my hands you think you're touching,
Rather two commas bent to give a pause,
Two beggars on the dusty pavement crouching
Past caring further now to plead their cause.

It is not my smile, expression lifting,
But exclamation-mark to end the line;
New emphasis, prejudiced and shifting
The customary meaning of the sign.

Nor is it my voice you think you're hearing —
A question-mark, unanswered, interfering.

LOST POEM

What happened to the poem that we made?
Shown in the index but not on the page,
As if it had its moment on the stage
And now remains a scene no longer played.

Can't find it in the poetry-book at all.
Torn out, the frayed edge leaves a mark.
Perhaps it's hidden under other work
Or in anthology more suitable?

Don't show it, if you find it, to your friends:
They would not understand its garbled tongue,
The words are rather difficult and long,
And you know how pathetically it ends.

I'll make a perfect haiku on my own
That former poem never need be known.

CREDITS

The love I loved, without once taking back
A part in part when direly torn apart;
The days I dazed with dismal, stricken heart,
Imagining you dead; bleak night's attack
Of dreams denoting death with no escape;
Hour's blood waiting; chronic prayers
For angels to have charge of your despairs
Winging every shadow into shape
Of Nature: My generating spirit
Spiralled in your life: Grant so much credit!

What you devalue has intrinsic worth
And shall be stored by me, restored to me
Through other eyes and lives, another birth
Harvesting mercy out of misery.

DEBITS

For debit I acknowledge keen delight
Of eye, of ear, inspired intelligence;
Belief in beauty's truth and permanence,
Images of magic, fancy's flight;
Extraordinary joy in being loved
For nothing but my own rhapsodic soul:
And loving in return I made you whole,
Self-deprecation handsomely disproved . . .

We rolled together down a steep incline,
One mind, one body toppled down the hill
In sudden playfulness, spontaneous passion.
Now separate we make a strange design,
Abused and ridiculed for matching ill —
Our poem out-of-date and out-of-fashion.

BIRTHDAY WISH

For all the wishes, flowers, I cannot send,
For all the kisses, hours, we cannot spend
Together: may this card alone attend
You on your birthday, greet and not offend
You. May Apollo and the Muses lend
You favours that the very gods intend
Shall evermore be yours; bend, condescend,
Touch, heal, misericorda mildly mend;
Orchestral angels solemnly ascend
By day and night, from sorrow to defend
You: With my every word that I have penned
You, I can nevermore attempt, pretend
My love is less than love that will transcend
All lesser loves: My love world without end.

ANOTHER BIRTHDAY

Your birthday hour has struck as midnight turns
The calendar into another day.
The magus of my watching heart discerns
Your star, which blazed upon my destiny,
No longer poised above that Bethlehem
Where I laid all my treasure at your crib,
But flickering around Jerusalem
Now paying court to pharisee or scribe.

That you were born was once my highest bliss
But now I wish I never had been born.
I would not greet you with a single kiss
Who celebrate with others, while I mourn.

Whatever angels now may blow your trumpet
Cover your ears! Then harken to my sonnet!

CLASSICAL FORM

Express your life in Latin or in Greek,
Wear borrowed thought fashioned in ancient time,
Let apt quotations sprinkle all you speak
To give your pettiness an air sublime;
Be careful to reveal great scholarship,
In experience find these layers of learning;
They lend authority, but fail to keep
You constant; add lustre to the yearning
For your reflection in the shining pool
Of my unfathomed love, but nothing more:
You tell me now yourself I was a fool —
Worshipped the beauty you were haggling for:

The Greeks, who lived the poems that they wrought
Cannot live ours: And ours has come to nought.

DO NOT APOLOGISE

You feel you must apologise for love?
To clear your conscience of unwanted load?
Regret the trouble caused, bad form you showed
In loving one you knew you could not have?

You did not notice the reserved label?
Bathsheba took hers off to wash, and lost
Her husband, not her heart, in the fable;
Her feelings were not counted in the cost.

Diana, not the huntress hard and chaste,
But of Poitiers the gracious lady,
The young king's life-long love, was not outfaced
By any scheming Catherine of Medici.

Do not apologise for love, but hate
That self-regard which is Love's apostate.

HARD AND FAST

There is no hard and fastness in my love
Hard rules to keep
Hard man to reap
Whoever sows in hollow or in grove.

No fastnesses enclosing mine and thine
Snatching want
Pruned plant
Withering in a word or look malign . . .

My love is void yet ever overflows
Invisible yet coiling into form
Untouchable, ascending as it goes
Into the paradise it floated from.

So loosely, lovely, broken, integral
Lavished, spilt, used up, a cruse of oil.

POETIC SENSE

I did not lack in love and all I gave
Increases my capacity for love;
By losing my contentedness I save
A rapture that no pedant dare reprove.

My happiness discarded, laid aside,
I take the garment of eternal woe;
You now put on a coat of borrowed pride —
It may not warm you in the winter snow.

The Muse will not despise my lowliness,
Will feed and clothe me with unfailing ardour;
For you I fear and for your callowness
Which swaggers in an artificial grandeur:

If you repudiate poetic sense
Your wisdom will construe as ignorance.

CRUCIFIED

When you fastened your cross around my neck
You made me accept it. 'This must be yours,'
You said, 'because I love you for ever.'

From the first I was reluctant to take
Something so precious. But when Love implores
We accept the gift as the giver.

'Again and again I clasp you,' you said.
I wore the pendant, its shaft a sword.
It burdened my breast like the albatross
With weight of love I could never shed.

Or was I hanging while nails were hammered?
Did I suffocate on your cross?

Forgive him. He knows not what he has done:
Agape crucified, Eros lives on.

REFLECTIONS ON WAKING: EASTER DAY

I have no god: as prophet call me false.
The god of Love triumphs not, but fails.
I shall not utter now the tones so dear.
Darkness and death I'm hoping for.

Break my limbs lest I again awake
To slow strangulation of the snake,
The crucifixion of another day
And desperation at my death's delay.

If Easter means arising, let me lie.
The god of Hate and Fear jealously
Devours with flames his altars saturated,
For Love has not been loved or vindicated.

The God I worship died as other men.
His suffering broke out and rose again.

LAST ATTEMPT

These poems are my last attempt to tell
You that I love you and will never cease.
Through them my misery has sought release.
Cathartic? Purgatory? To hell with Hell!

I would bombard you with them like bullets
Exploded from my loaded pent-up grief,
Except I know it would not bring relief —
You would shrug them off as paper pellets.

'What more do you expect' I hear you say.
'Friendship? Occasionally a social call?'
More or less from nothing's grand total
Leaves no remainder in respects to pay.

Whatever life may bring or chance may hold
Think of me lovingly when you are old.

LOVE'S REASONING

My ink is dry and my invention spoiled:
I wish to die: no poem can I make.
Like Petrarch without Laura in the world
My loss awakes within me when I wake
Each day; The plague took Laura from him,
An act of God? You took yourself from me
And scoffed at my complaint in Reason's name.
But Reason turns against such blasphemy,
Unites with Love to draw us into God.
There is a Reason of the heart which tells
How Love is forced to carry its own load,
The very instrument by which it falls.

According then to Reason Love must die,
And since I truly love you, so must I.

CODA: MISUNDERSTANDING

You have mythologised my mind
and think thereby you understand,
believing your own myth about me
until you can no longer doubt me:
all my lies are plain to see —
my deceit, hypocrisy.

All that I can say, explain
to contradict you, is in vain.
I know myself — till you confuse me.
I am not what you will suppose me.
Keep your myth, I cannot live it,
if sometime I may forgive it.

Myths describe the mind that makes them:
the real other always breaks them.
You keep your god, describe the world
in terms that leave your myth unspoiled.
I must escape to find my soul,
the destiny that makes me whole.

EPILOGUE

THE GARDENER

To the Gardener, who, making paradise,
Radiates sweet, seasonal advice,
Who loves me when I laugh,
Whose rod and staff
Have saved me in the valley, brought me near
The fountain flowing into water clear,
Who sailed me out of harbouring my grief
Into summer — the tall ash in leaf:

Waves, oceans, shores, philosophy and song,
The round world's endless roundelay of wrong,
Storm, winter, mud, acrimony, censure, —
Yet riding through them all the dear adventure
Of poem-life, written in the living:
This sonnet is my gesture of thanksgiving.

OUR PROPER DARK

HAIKU

Candles in dark church
Stars in darker night
Light of God in darkest heart.

REVERIE

If my poetic self is brought to mind
reflected in your consciousness,
half a phrase or touch,
book lent with love,
you do me truly more than favours.

Days are lost in worldness and we
then lose each other whom we know
only in the fusion
of two reveries
whose transience attains the real.

The functions of the brain are all events,
a festival, a mêlée
of cooperating cells,
which interact and keep
a carnival in constancy.

How can I remember I'm a poet
or keep becoming one anew
unless I catch flambuoyance
of your recognition,
my poetry alight from yours?

WHAT USE ARE POETS?

(Und wozu Dichter in dürftiger Zeit?)
title from Hölderlin

Alcaic Ode

In parsimonious times who will plead for poets
When bread and circuses must be paramount?
    Expediency makes tall excuses
        Debts do not die, nor residual hunger.

Our human life is dear and we pay the toll
By pining slowly starved of Parnassian grass
    That goats will crave and sheep discover
        Sweeter than flowers in polluted meadow.

It is for their dear life, and not theirs alone
That poets write, whose unknown petitioners
    Will draw abundant strength they need from
        Generous gamblers with life worth living.

Not use perhaps, but wont, gives the poet room
But cannot place him save as a therapist.
    Repairs are not his task, but making
        Worlds out of words without recreation.

AEROPLANES AT NIGHT

Alcaic Ode

The aeroplanes flew over in darkest space −
Their roar was louder heard in the hush of night,
    Lit up in starry outline like a
        Skeleton, luminous, heading westward.

They kept formation, each one above the next −
Direction, speed, together in perfect time
    But only light-shape, trav'lling sound-stream
        Sensible, all the construction hidden.

A pattern lit by love as it shows me up
Is all that can be seen of my voyaging
    When tedious body weight and daily
        Selfhood is lost in surrounding darkness.

And you, who fly with me, alongside but high
Above the earth to destiny ever dark,
    The keeping course our only order −
        Light answers light, nor do engines falter.

15

TOURNAMENT

Asclepiadic Ode

War requires us to arm: Love is another case
Where once warriors brave moved in their heavy mail
    Now the harness confronts us
    Empty, clean disembowelled within.

Slits at neck and at groin: there the sharp arrows find
Entrance far into flesh, piercing to artery,
    Causing blood to erupt and
    Drain the skin of its inward sap.

Walking past hollow visors with their sightlessness,
Knowing throes of the love enemies found they felt
    Even dealing the death blow
    Honour never in jeopardy.

Where, I ask, then is mine? Helmet and chained cuirass?
God's provision has failed: devils may beat retreat;
    Love prevails over every
    Kind of armoured accoutrement:

Having struck us alive, all that was dead in us,
Caused the bloodstream to flow spilling upon the earth,
    Leaves the life that had risen
    Dead once more without remedy.

FREEING THE CAPTIVES

Asclepiadic Ode

Set the prisoners free, each captivated hurt,
Asculepius waits; healing is found with him.
   Loneliness is a fortress
   Manned with plans that have come to nought.

Nature, music, art, silence and solitude
These are balms but not cures; onward we march our life
   Through the death that beseiges
   Inescapably everywhere.

Therapies may do good; tell us to cry aloud,
Mourn the self that has died, ravaged by sheer neglect:
   Raised to consciousness slightly
   Learns to weep without showing it.

Those who love us will think this recovery.
Misery can play tricks, make out a rational case.
   We pretend we can manage,
   Blind ourselves to such recklessness.

Why not deploy this stroke, take it another way?
Suffering digs the well; water begins to flow;
   Others find it and use it,
   Those who crawl along parched with dust.

Go then, tyrants and slaves; torturers, stand at ease!
Death is welcome; delay proves less acceptable.
   No more pain is admitted;
   In or outside, I set it free.

TETHERED

Asclepiadic Ode: Crete

Tethered like an old donkey to a flowery ledge
So the village is tied fast to the mountain slope.
    Upward terraces green their
    Grade to shape of the trees and rocks.

Motor-bikes in the night: youths on them lash about:
Not in Psychro where Zeus came from the womb of the earth:
    Damp fecundity hidden,
    Caved beneath the most lofty crags.

Snowy-headed he rests, rearing above the world,
Solemn now and reposing, with his youthful zest,
    Ancient urge to create, for-
    Gotten, quaintly magnanimous.

Lizard, orchid and thorn, country of wrinkled folk;
These continue his work, guarding both earth and sky,
    Pommes de terre et de ciel, with
    Almond-blossom for melling bees.

Moon and stars are in space: we are alongside them,
Lucent over the plateau as if over earth.
    Spray of cockcrow uplifts us,
    Wave of dawn washes over us,

Each is tethered, and I know I am leashed to pain;
None aware among those watching me walk the world.
    Black-clad people resume their
    Tasks, and climb up the winding street.

'WHERE YOU SEE NOTHING THERE YOUR GODS DWELL'

(title is a quotation from Hölderlin)

Sapphic Ode

Gods cannot be traced by investigation,
Time and space determine our very vision.
We have let these concepts control our thinking
Govern our living.

Let us start again without definitions.
All the lines we rule that divide the soma:
Past and present, future and world unending
Meet in our psyche.

Peace, we know, is simply to keep the balance,
Not to panic: changes are meant to happen,
Life demands them. We can envisage wholeness
In and beyond us.

Sappho, Dido, choirs of creative women,
Heard or unheard, do not be wayward! Challenge
Endless pros and cons and unreal devotion,
Powers and glories!

Holy is the dwelling of gods and humans.
Categories cleave our experience, leave us
Clutching bits and pieces and wondering why we
Never feel even.

Ours is vision, ours the transforming spirit.
We can risk at last what our hearts desire and
Love each other, knowing it's what we're made for,
Makes us immortal.

THE ECSTASY OF ST TERESA (BERNINI)

How dare the angel smile
as he inflicts the wound,
executing orders with detachment,
        almost pleasure?
Ah — he is only messenger
cannot choose, refuse,
        (little Nazi!)

Hail Teresa!
Torso meagre
hidden by engulfing cloak,
serge, heavy-woven;
foot and hanging hand
signal your surrender.

For ever will your agony endure
from this penetration,
though your quickened moans may die away.
Some will harshly warn you,
others try to cure you,
but that torn heart
will throw you
from wave to fiery wave,
a slip of coracle,
until you achieve the resting-point
where spear becomes space,
        pain becomes peace,
with flames a circling halo.

ANY OLD WOMAN

'After a recitative
denoting her distress
Berenice sings an aria
in which she begs to die
rather than live
without the love of Titus.'

In dignified tones
a Radio Three announcer
introduces the theme:

I am on my knees
in the kitchen
as the flood of music over me
washes the despair
of Berenice
round my wall, my heart.

'Such emotion', I think,
'should be trapped in art . . .
not let loose
with all apparent nonchalance
into any old kitchen
any old women'.

ATTENDING DEATH

Little old ladies
in separate houses
waiting to die
no knowing the day
or hour of darkness
when ultimate weakness
demands the surrender
of built-up character.

Each one alone —
while will to go on
shall last — may be seen
in her daily routine.

Who can discover
a regiment braver
or hermit more holy
without melancholy?

When it is my turn
I'll blow out the lantern —

Even now as I think
bending over the sink
my tears down the drain
are leaving no stain

Once death is over
who may recover!

FOOL AND ANGEL ENTERING THE CITY

(painting by Cecil Collins)

Fool and Angel wander hand in hand
beyond the city walls:
The poet is a fool at court,
and angels something only fools believe in.
Both of us were both of these
in one coherent being.

Once you loved my harlequin ideas,
my starry tidings.
Once you clowned beside me
cap o' bells a-jingle
pinions charged to fly.

Now you have settled in the city
I shall never enter
across the huge moat between us.
I stand chequered
by the squared portcullis:
you more distant than angels
and I merely foolish.

INDIAN WOMEN AT WINDERMERE

Indian women at Windermere
why carry plastic buckets and pans
stooped and bending low,
when you know
how to sail along like swans
your loads aloft as head-gear?

Oldish women in walking-shoes,
saris, coats and spectacles,
with wealthy, westernised sons
Indians
living in modern bungalows —
how much of yourselves have you had to lose?

If I were you I would wish to be
inconspicuous yet walking tall;
no slavery
to nationality
whether in Britain or Bengal —
head high and both hands free.

LOST LOVE

He who lives is not the one I knew —
the man I loved has died, or lives no more —
a false persona overcame the true.

A year I sought him chasing any clue
would lead me to my love beheld before,
for he who lives is not the one I knew.

The circling maze of Hades I passed through
in case my love was lost upon that shore,
whose false persona overcame the true.

Among the living sometimes one or two
I'd glimpse perhaps who faint resemblance bore,
but none who lives can be the one I knew.

With hollow sobbing I could scarce subdue
I mourned my love, whom nothing would restore,
whose false persona overcame the true.

I keep his image safe from common view,
deep within my own most hidden core,
for he who lives is not the one I knew,
a false persona overcame the true.

THE REBEL

In the name of study
and for the sake of knowledge
we encourage children
to press flowers,
pin butterflies.

In the name of study
and for the sake of knowledge
brilliant scientists
experiment with animals
pin-point the stuff of life.

'How dare you press a snowdrop,
a living thing?'
wept the child, little knowing
how soon she would herself be pressed
in the hard-backed pages
of education.

But when I observe
how much wire
and what miles of iron and steel
are required
to pin down the human spirit
and that it still flowers −

I take hope −
and move paper wings,
open desiccated petals
in the love released
by this tiny rebel.

BALLAD OF THE BEREAVED

I went to the doctor
desiring to die
was told 'Come back later,
we're busy today'.

Crept back later
and told my pain
which gets no better
drives me insane.

'Where does it hurt?'
inquired the doctor.
'In head, in heart,
in psyche, soma'.

'We have no cure
for what you describe,
you must endure
I cannot prescribe.

Time will heal
it never fails,
Time will seal
with crabbéd scales.'

'Thank you', I said
and turned away,
while hours bleed
through another day.

When we are young
Time is slow
a year is long;
we soon outgrow

Losses, cramp,
stabbing wound –
we raise our lamp
on pearls new-found:

But Time is short
when we are old
and pain thus caught
is never healed.

TREES IN WINTER SUNLIGHT

Leaning pale
against the hill
in this long lenten fast
tall trunks intangible
cast shadows on the slope
sinister, substantial.

Shadow
more real
than substance –
and the cause of this reversal:
winter.

Half-hearted sun
casts a twitch of smile
across the woods
where frost unmelted
seals the sap.

Leaning pale
against the hill
all my substance gone
heavy, sinister,
sloping, shadowy
into this hard ground,
forced
into a season of austerity.

SHADOW SELF – COMPOSING

Shadow, I have cast you
over flames
and stones of the hearth

You rock sideways
head in hands

I lean away
and am delivered of you
faithless one

But wait!

My hand on white page
is defined in shade

I stop, raise it, look –
five fingers and a pen
which writes
not what they indicate
but what you
dark self
dictate

rocking sideways over
mind's flame
stones of syntax
head in hands.

SCHOENBERG'S VERKLÄRTE NACHT

Let night between us fall aside
in pools of forgiveness
leaving moonlight only where we walk . . .

Doubts slowly drain away
in shadows of the forest
leaving palest clarity around us . . .

Where we stumbled darkly
in tears, untouching,
suddenly we now behold each other . . .

Trees that lowered over us
are transformed into guardians
who comprehend our suffering . . .

Ah now I see I love you
not under cover of the branching night
but beneath its candelabra . . .

LIFE SICKLE

I
Heaven forbade
that I forbid
the blade
that cuts
to quicken
all that bleeds,
ripens, seeds.

II
Soil and soul,
porous, humus;
no clay
impervious.

III
Tares, tears,
the hundredfold ears
of wheat that die
and come to mind
first-fruits cordial
pentecostal
of kardia
lifted-up.

IV

No burnt-flesh
petted calf,
fatted
offered up
on abstract altar
to devouring concrete statues
of no stature.

V

What appears incarnate
is ensouled;
when complete
full height
bows, bends,
ends.

FEBRUARY NIGHT

Cold strides
leagues deep.
How he boots it
strikes heel sans mercy
sets hibernal pincer
columns in ambush
to nip dare-devil budding
rigor-black at edge!

I rise in night.
He has glaciated panes.
Owls duetting keen,
skate thin layers of sound —
they thirst for blood.

I wake thirsty,
saliva hardened on the tongue like rime.
The beaked-ones will pierce me,
eyes upon me
Athene!
How long till morning?
Hours, days, years?
And the sun's retrieval
in pale, aching light?

Transform the world once more
sidereal candle!
Starry helium
heal our wounds of winter!

NIRVANA: SNOW IN SPRING

Sun shines in Spring
but every flower that tries to grow
is smothered in continual snow
of pain.

Accustomed seasons change
but I am learning how to die,
remain in winter without cry
for Spring.

Flower of hope brings hurt
reminding of the hopes I had:
not until such dream is dead
will pain

finally achieve
the full oblation now required
releasing me from once desired
Spring.

RAVINE

Without great pain I would have no remainder
Of that love I lived in for a season.
As exiles bear remembrance of a home
They cannot see, yet never leave in vision,
A continuing place, although more real,
For clear Imagination recreates
The daily dance of its reality . . .
So I shall ever carry my exile.

Without a landmark countryside is waste;
Without a signpost, insignificance.
The earth betrays her former land or sea
By tiny shells or dainty plant-impressions,
Remnants of some mountain-forming force
Like Love, which gouged a deep ravine,
Sheer-sided, narrow, striking through my land.
Perhaps some healing herb, or hardy shrub
May fasten on the rock-face, barely hide
The precipice. In time I will avoid
It on my daily walks, using well-worn
Footpath, lane and style. Yet even these
Keep twisting back and round again and down
To where I stumble in great pain alone.

SPRING EQUINOX

Breezes danced the mist away all night
and none could sleep
but curtains open
welcomed early light and unexpected song
from birds of jubilation.

With all the world in balance now and turning
to toss and turn
is only natural,
to know the revolutionary universe
pivot upon the mind.

Equanimity is not for us:
male and female
numbers alternate
and tiny contradictions wrestle in the dark
rhapsodic for repose.

Branches now are orgulous with buds
on every twig
the thick of generation —
what equilibrium in a feather blown of hope
against the boundary wall?

LOAVES AND FISHES

Loaves and fishes of Love
perpetually make fragments.
The utmost we bring
the more may be consumed:
and scraps for all.

'Thank you' Easterners say,
'for the basket of your presence'
to a visitor.
What richer gift than gathered-up
Love's fragments for a friend?

A whole loaf, entire fish
may have once existed
are worth imagining,
but when the press is on us
pity crumbles them.

Broken Love is shareable:
one world among so many
can go round.
Our particles are cosmic
and our fragments wild with life.

Coherence is not simple:
multiple division makes more shares
or more to share?
Love is never enough and yet
we take each morsel gladly.

It looks a mess, a waste
but a multitude was fed,
and such a feast
is bound to make left-overs.

Won't you take my basket?

FUTURE NOW

This poem is dedicated to my
friend, inspiration and critic
BRENDON THOMAS,
who, at the height of his powers,
died suddenly on 27th August 1983.

An exceptional person

Teilhard de Chardin thought people could be divided
Into those who say 'yes' to the future and those who say 'no'.
That was before the bomb whose existence is a negation
And now a 'yes' to the future has to be 'no'.
This world: mountain, river, prairie, ocean, city
Is worth our affirmation, not for speed,
Not for size, longevity, beauty or for strength,
But for ideas, crucial, exceptional people,
Like Coleridge who took in Helvellyn on the way
To visiting Wordsworth, twelve pens in his knapsack
A book of German poems and a cravat!

People could be divided into those who prefer the sea
And those who choose to live among trees and hills:
Expansive imaginations that reach to far horizons
And secluded souls who centre inward:
Those who believe in the future ride on will-power, vision
To put to sea in ships they have built themselves,
Find and explore the unknown always beyond their sight,
Learning from experience just too late:
Others lie on the beach, tide in tide out, convinced
Nothing new ever happens under the sun:
Each of us is sections of everyone.

The sea is rhythm. Rhythm in trees is slow but more
Related to form. Trees are exceptional people.
They do not have to try to prove or improve themselves,
Nor do they cease continual rings of growth.
They lose their leaves without any fuss, storing in roots
The sap that rises again for all it's worth;
Belonging fully to earth but living also in sky
They have no death but only transformations.
The life of tide and tree conflict, contend within us;
Exceptional people find a harmony,
Their ebb and flow contained in onward spiral.

Mary said 'yes' to the future, possible god *and* man.
She was a very *un*-exceptional woman:
Who mostly suffer life in labour giving birth
To Love, which then inevitably dies,
Condemned by the world whose atmosphere it makes,
Degraded by the fear of transformation.
We need not worship the woman: she moves in tide and tree.
We need not worship the world, or even Love.
The rhythm of 'yes' and 'no' will find an ultimate form,
And having found it let go and begin again.
A 'yes' to the future has to be obstinate!

ANTHROPOS IN THE ICE-AGE

Nothing comes between
my cottage and the moon
save the ash-tree's arms
and a mountain domed with firs.

No dint upon the snow
within my curve of hill
save robin and *lapin* —
a wide, white margin.

Now I appear and enter:
clothed in cottage
shaded from the moon
attend my fireside shrine.

These footsteps to the door
show anthropos is here
feebly warm, intelligent,
pontifical, magnificent.

WINTER WISHES

I want my winter to go on, my blizzard walks,
my rambling to and fro, unlike the sheep who face
together always in the same direction,
snow or sun.

The faces of the sheep are white as shining clowns
in the sun. They take it easy lying down
like clustered mushrooms in gestation on the
pregnant field.

They turn toward Spring: that is their direction.
They wait for gales and damp and shortages to cease
yet slowly fatten in the barren winter fields
great with lambs.

On all sides Spring invades us like a devastation.
The lambs will not keep silent, nor face in one direction.
They shine in unprotected patchy hope,
new born.

We protect ourselves behind glass and pavements
from Spring, meeting devastation with a sneer.
The city rocks on multifarious nature,
soft as earth.

And I am soft as earth; all you see my city.
And I am great with shining unborn substances,
yet all you see the blizzard walks of my
winter wishes.

A DEEP BUT DAZZLING DARKNESS

HAIKU

In every country
Trees mark the land
Seasons mark the trees —
We walk on.

LOVE NIGHTS

Foeda est in coitu et brevis voluptas.

PETRONIUS

You claim that lust gives
           brief delight
But love can last all night.

Love-nights are seldom,
           few and rare
Since who can fully share

An enigmatic
           hidden self
For long without relief?

The body soon will
           slump to sleep
Unless we singly keep

Awake, and tuned
           to more than song,
To love that lasts life-long.

AN OUTSIDER'S VIEW

You make a life from life within the tribe
and enervate the little ones you serve.
No babes and sucklings now — get rid of them,
and give yourself a rest from parenting,
a chance to answer other claims suppressed
too long, like Hopkins in his piety.

You forged your family in the flinty world,
not round the hearth of ancestors and kin.
Let them go forth and make their own new niche
as different from yours as they would wish,
without apology, regret or guilt,
or even frequently reporting back.

They'll come to know themselves, alone, unique,
aware of diverse creatures on the earth
and loves that come before the ties of blood;
devotion to a destiny that drives
beyond the totem god and his great clutch
of pecking worshippers; beyond and yet
within the mind's fine eye, the heart's strong sense,
as founder of strange future dynasties.

THE NEW IS BEING FORMED

Call it Life:
it is Pre-Death.
It hurts like hell
to tremble continually by the well
of weeping,
to scan the unthinkable future
for sign of fire or cloud,
to release the unbearable past
the plagues we caused
the slavery we suffered.

Too dark, too close.
The promised land after forty years?
New nativity?
Between pangs the respites are too short.

Some retreat to Pre-Death calm,
flesh-pots of self-righteousness:
'We took a wrong-turning
it led into the wilderness'.

The new is being formed within our hardihood
soft as milk and honey.
That will be After-Death:
that will be Life.

ENLOVEMENT

Let us write our blind words:
they come from pure light
into criss-cross darkness
of labyrinthine logic.

Let us build with sharp words:
they share our cutting light
until bludgeoned
blunted at the edge
by tools of bleak analysis.

Hear my new words:
I did not want — no
'a husband and a lover'.
I did not try — no
'to have my cake and eat it'.
I did not think — no
I could 'have it both ways'.

My experience is beyond
these besotted clichés:
nothing men (or little women) say
applies to how I love.
I am not set on sex
nor do I prefer platonic friendships.
When I love
I feel myself dare-hearted
I sense my own embeautiment
I know the full philander of the human.

When I belove this man
encherish that woman
con-soul some child,
we, in our mutual
ideal ambience
transform the brutal world,
suffer its realities
with adoration, laughter,
and clear, sharp enlovement.

MY BODY MYSELF

Pure am I as white sands of the West
open, expansive contour of sloping shore . . .

Hollowed by wind sheering over my surface
with fractured shells, pebbles of felspar . . .

Rain and sun take turns to lave and sear me
scour my serpentine and mica jewels . . .

Fluent tide-return straggling seaweed
reveals me jade and turquoise below waves . . .

Alone — frequented by cormorant
one coracle of saints per thousand years . . .

Spread your arms, barefooted swiftly run
over abrasive sand to freezing seas . . .

Once of a summer day I shall be warmed
alive with white, brilliant, brittle heat . . .

Lie and run me through your fingers then
or wading, follow me beyond your depth.

MIND'S DESIRE

You cannot penetrate my secret space
With so-called love in search of an orgasm,
Esprit and corps kept in a separate place,
Head and penis marked by dualism.
I want your seeds of thoughtful protoplasm —
To reach my burning omphalos within,
Your recklessness and skill to dare the chasm
Leading to my holiest domain.
There I shall feast you more than food and wine,
Which lull the very potency I need
To open up most precious gifts of mine
Sealed, imprisoned, waiting to be freed.

I give your thoughts my bodily conception
Desire you with consummate intellection.

PLATONIC SOUL-STUDY

the amorousnesse of an harmonious soule.

DONNE

The Greeks maintained no celibacy of soul
but harnessed steeds as for a chariot race
with charioteer, as an harmonious whole:

two or five together keeping pace
neck by neck and flaring nostrils wide
cornering with swift and skilful grace.

Patroclus and his horses, gentle-eyed,
drove to a death intended for another
to rally those who feared or turned aside,

yet his stallions mourned him as a brother —
So fled my soul when all its reins were loose,
the horses rearing on without a driver.

The battle lasted years, no lull, no truce,
when my soul-steeds could find no part to play,
bereft of charioteer they were no use:

sunk beneath the sea in bronze he lay
until dredged up and set upon his feet,
and prized in the museum on display.

Straight and stiff his tunic's flowing pleat,
hard the curve of rein in broken hand
with white and glassy eyes for counterfeit.

Gone his steeds that galloped on the strand —
and souls live not by charioteer alone
but harmonised, obeying love's command:

driver, wheels and horses, three in one,
mind and matter moved with energy
another circuit valiantly begun,

achieving with consummate artistry
cosmic order, virtue, passion, power,
an excellence of love most real and rare.

UNEVEN LOVE

All night she sat and sewed the hem of her skirt,
tacked and stitched, measured, unpicked,
it wouldn't come even.

All night ridiculous, foolish thoughts pricked
in and out of her mind like needle and thread
but wouldn't come straight.

The soft, black wool was ruckled, gathered too thick;
hacked about, it would never hang well:
she had made a mistake.

Better to undo it all and shake it free;
better to smooth every seam from her mind
of this uneven love.

At last she put it aside, abandoned, half-done;
a waste of time; they never work out
these adaptations.

But she wakes to sudden, uneven pain in her heart —
tacked and stitched, measured, unpicked,
and then abandoned.

MISFATE

We thought we met by chance.
Then, grateful that our lives should fall
within one span of time and space
or overlap at all,
we called it fortune.

We made our meetings then
across the world and seasons,
believing in some greater destiny.

Now chance has changed to hazard,
fortune to disaster.

To avoid coincidence —
our paths like scissors crossing —
we make precise provision
not to meet by chance,
lest unlikelihood consign us
impossibly to fate.

TO EROS

Don't you realise
I am old?
My Athens a north-
ern city, cold
unmerciful
to passion?

Here lie no meadows where love may graze
(the boy-scouts play there).
Here no mountains oozing anemones,
but crags and tended golf-courses.
Here no halcyon, no fluted bay,
no Aphrodite rising from the Forth
only mists and promontories
and spray of screaming birds.

Alas the heart
is always Hellas
and since you
leapt across
my cobbles
I find I am
blue, hazy, shining,
mediterranean and
focus of every force
that swept
the shore-line of the human.

LIKE A LOAD OF LOGS

(title from Hölderlin's Mnemosyne)

Too much is too difficult
like a load of logs on the shoulders
strapped to the bent-horizontal back.

Too many too jealous and chafe the neck.

Consciousness too complex:
   if other means of transport
   were invented
   for cumbersome world-freight
   logs of hard-dealing,
   new side-effected suffering
   would increase the burden
   and with old orders gone
   there would be no remedy.

Too little can be decided:
whether again to mend a conforming a sandal,
risk the pinch of new
or horn our feet for nakedness?
Where to lean the load
the dyke crumbling?
Can we lay it down, put it aside,
straighten a while
and resume the human?

All must be accounted for in time.

Across the marshy glen
is it owls that are flying
short-eared in daylight?
And are those patron peaks
to be prized as wasteland
or conserved for nuclear waste?

Is it a case of continuing
beside the burn between the boulders
picking each forward step?
Or should those be praised
who freak ahead
drop down dead in their ruts
harnessed and heavy-laden?

45

Like women
must we keep stopping for children
tie a lace, stroke a flower,
sun an hour in the heather
or strive for shelter
turn our backs on sleet?

Have we no cap or hood
to pull down over the ears
in the severing windstream?
Did we set out too early
or have we begun a journey
whose end is already too late?

Too much is too difficult.

To each according to his servitude.

The holy man escapes
who begets no dependents
eats gifts and fosters detachments.

       *   *   *

We see the load on our friends
notice where it presses,
how the straps cannot be slackened
nor the neck unstiffened.
We find where footmarks have circled:
(they have no sense of direction
who cannot look up).
Hands hang limp
or clutch any support.
Knees are not enfeebled but deformed
by such long portering.

Our own load we cannot see,
nor know exactly the contents
of our consignment.
We can bear the trivia
on a little finger
but the dead weight
what is that
which cannot be shifted,
prevents our shifting?
Are we shiftless then to weep so?

We adore the open road
but some invisible
hard, non-locatable,
broken, sharp pain
leadens the load.

An enemy has done this,
slipped it onto us
when we were passing cheerfully.

Or we suspect a friend –
the one we trusted most and loved
when we set down our burdens
at the crossroads,
surveyed the various routes
and gazed ahead
like Romans on the Wall
at the beautiful barbarity we longed for
but dared not.

We follow up the sheep track
in single file
slower and stumbling more
at every false summit.

Too much is too difficult
like a load of logs on the shoulders
and never now for the hearth.

MY TROY

I am my own Cassandra and foresee
the fall of my own Troy —
    murder of the heroes
    destruction of her children
    women taken as spoils.

None can save Troy now — the very gods
are scuttling in retreat.
    She brought the dummy horse
    within her sacred space —
    it spilled out all its spite.

She was deceived and ransacked utterly
by Greek aggrandisement.
    Her altars now are fallen
    golden treasures stolen
    palaces in flames.

Helen now has lost her queenliness
her beauty and her youth.
    She lives to end her life.
    The brutal brothers both
    now lord it over us.

Cressida has been flung to and fro
between opposing warriors
    who mock her now, since she
    preferred their manhood
    to the cause they fought.

Your victory Achilles shall be short
but Troy's defeat eternal.
    Her suffering shall be sung
    whenever human worth
    is slain and trampled on.

I am my own Cassandra and foresee
my death in Mycenae.
    No place for the displaced.
    We dwell within our sorrow
    in every earthly kingdom.

STATIONS OF THE CROSS

Pilate washed his hands; foresaw
those who thirst for blood having to be appeased.
    Whether divine or human
    they present the lustral cup,
rhyton of death and the darker side of truth.

Truth is not a matter for
discussion when a cross has to be carried
    proportioned beyond our strength
    shouldered in the knowledge
that Truth itself is bound and in league with death.

Die like a king: he stumbles
weakly in front of women who watching weep.
    'Weep not for him, but ourselves
    and our little ones dying
like those killed in his stead by mercenaries.'

Veronica lifts her veil
cleans the blood and dirt gently from mouth and eyes
    as if for a child who had
    clutched her in need of comfort
whose hands were not free to wipe his own features.

Be sure there is no reprieve:
the straight horizontal wood burdens upon
    the doubled spine and hung head
    while the upward vertical
rests its angle over the shoulders we flogged.

Too much affliction prevents
the execution of orders. Our soldiers
    expedite the violent death,
    pressgang a stranger, ashamed
themselves to carry the dragging central shaft.

Is he almost glad to lie
stretched out, while we nail him through ankles and wrists?
    But lifted up it is pain
    prevails from on high, the reign
of Jesus of Nazareth, Love incarnate.

Before consciousness is lost
he speaks to his neighbours condemned on each side.
    Victims of poverty, they
    become co-victims with him
who takes away the sin of legal murder.

It is expedient that some
should be slaughtered to keep the law and the peace
    however innocent they,
    or guilty of compassion
touching the human as if it were divine.

He looks down on all mothers
and pities their brokenness as they attend
    the sacrifice of their sons
    permitted by his 'father'
the one we call 'good' and believe in as God.

Comrades are huddled around:
he beseeches John, his favourite, to care for
    his mother; for so we love
    that those we love should be close
and love us in each other when we are gone.

At last the suffocation
is nearly complete, and he roars in torment
    as his breath is surrendered
    in exhalation of pain —
This is how we extract the spirit by force.

Our soldiers cannot divide,
apportion the guilt in the garment he wore.
    We tear his flesh in its stead
    to ascertain it is dead:
the raiment the holy wove for the spirit.

Lowered again to earth and
below the earth, into the womb of Nature —
    How grotesque our expressions:
    for grief is not beautiful —
God and Man are not prettily wrenched apart.

WAYS AND MEANS

I'll sing of a charm of finches flying
In Autumn over the loch, defying
Gales that gather force.
Birches gold with silver, bracken
Tall and bending now to blacken,
Cry of wary grouse.
Water, sky, wood and moorland
Patch of cosmic pattern –
Man with woman hand in hand
Reconciled in passion.
No need here of greed here
Or duty beyond completion.
No stress of distress, for
We walk within our vision.

I can record computers clicking
Digits dotted, figures flicking
Bigger barns for facts
Assembled to be organised,
Averaged and analysed,
Statistical fuel-stacks.
The Archtool and calculator
Machine we can consult,
Perfected manipulator,
None to call a halt.
Can we choose or refuse?
Can the robot reason,
Stop to think on the brink,
Work out our salvation?

I recall the fable of La Fontaine,
Of Ant who scurried to store her grain
In summertime for winter;
Cicada through all summer played
Composing songs; but was repaid
With death by starving later.
And blind Homer begged for bread
in beauty-loving Hellas –
A world of ants would all be fed;
Grasshopper rule would kill us!
Under Plato or NATO
Must we live by bread alone?
We eat to live but live to give
The world its fill – of song.

FLOWERS OF FROST

Who can remember
in winter
flowers and foliage,
olive shadows, lucent lake,
corners of the garden quietly singing?
That was another age.

We lifted our countenance
to raindrops' hazy sustenance,
lingered amid the pillars,
uncovered revolution.

         *   *   *

Now spiky flowers of frost
bloom in every brittle diamond blade
of withered grass;
black waters run
beneath a smear of ice;
the fountain thickens
as she feeds the silent loch
whose surface shows opaque
unflinching eyes.

Pale gold
sloping fields
like burnished shields
face cold
mountainous distance
whose onslaught in the bloodstream
makes old
scars stand out whiter.

Warmth in old walls;
roots in deep earth;
life muted, stroked, held,
waits to be healed,
withdraws to hibernate
secluded, close, secret, intimate.

DARK NIGHT OF THE SPIRIT

Swords rust in attics
regarded antiquated
non-conducive to material satisfaction.

Mental fight requires the word-in-hand
that sleeps not in its sheath
but wreaks a spiritual havoc:

A havoc like the hurricane of spirit
Geist — full of rampant gusts
to blow us wildly off the beaten track.

The flame that lights our life
is spluttering for lack of oxygen:
inspiration comes in frantic gasps.

*   *   *

Dark, mature, wise woman,
hidden part of god, revealed
to those alone who love her;

No emaciated, professional 'ghost',
no father, son or virgin,
but *sophia*, black but comely.

Her favours will bring no high position
but parched, endless torment,
branded a troubadour.

Our song will be made welcome,
but we shall be cast out
from the castles of this world.

Our lady must disown us all the more
whom she will meet in secret.
Choose power then, or wisdom!

*   *   *

By night, O Nicodemus, you shall learn
of birth from god-the-Mother
if you watch while others sleep,

Nor put aside the sop she offers
bitter though it taste, sharp as betrayal:
the ultimate surrender: to be born.

Reward her ceaseless labour,
her great travail d'amour
to bring you where you may begin to breathe.

Reward her with your never-failing love,
your service in her cause,
your chariot racing through the realms of light.

She is the oxygen and you the flame;
she, the gale with tongues of fire
destroying our established habitations.

                 *   *   *

Run riot, *ruach*, through the world!
Let darkness cover us!
Our tombs will be deserted then at dawn.

UPSTREAM OF OURSELVES

Despite the current that tows us temporally
down, forces us
into invincible age,
loosens our rocks,
nudges the safest way
is to go, flow,
keep in the midstream
show no violence
against the rapids . . .

our source of strength is upstream

and in confronting the river
we make a friction that generates
an art of exaltation;
we work the will our conviction demands
part under water swimming ferociously,
part determined to breathe.

We push towards a destiny
dreamed as possible,
ante-perceived, admired,
realised ahead of memory.

We steadfastly set our face
towards tranquillity
where birches drink and cress is plentiful,
where snow melts in shadow
and birds belong to either element.

It is upstream of ourselves
and we shall have made our end.

RESTORATION

Trees lean over from Eden and yearn for Earth.
Spirits that buffet them are wild and ruthless.
Everything in Eden is out of hand
since the humans left.
Gods of destruction rule there, gods of excess.
Trustful, gentle creatures, delicate plants,
mediatory insects, world-haunting birds
have become extinct.

'Adam where are you?' cries Yahweh, his motherhood roused,
'I repent of my senseless fury in driving you out.
I never should have expected blind subservience
to petty laws.
Return again and I'll treat you differently,
respect the complex, curious nature I gave you.
We shall be partners and you shall have a say
in the overall plan.

'Eve, dear Eve, do not harden your heart
against me for ever: though I confess the hurt
you and your daughters have suffered for centuries
may never heal.
Despite the inhuman way I evicted you
in your helplessness, return, with your hard-won knowledge
of good and ill; of good that is never complete,
and impending death.'

         *   *   *

'Mother-God: you have come to awareness too late.
we cannot return to our childhood home and your
benevolent tyranny: We cannot restore
the ancient garden.
The harm you did us is irredeemable
and we have settled on Earth, all over the earth
in uneasy co-existences. You may
visit us.

'Or, if the gates are opened, we and you
shall cross the forbidden border to an fro,
and this futile separation, this either/or
may come to an end.
Then Eden and Earth may slowly replenish each other,
discover the balance that has for so long been lost.

Our science will find a way to prevent the chaos
you cannot control.

'You may create new fruits, herbs, flowers,
new holiness in the climate of the spirits —
and we shall rest, deep under smiling trees
in conversation.
We shall converse in new awareness of love,
adoring each other's worthship, beauty, skill,
unafraid of the serpent who meant no harm,
unafraid of death.

'Life and death we shall hold in our daily hands,
shaping each one, appreciating the forms
that each can take when we make them incarnate
within ourselves.'

      *   *   *

The gates are open in Eden, the guard removed —
gods and humans come and go as they will —
precarious spirits are balanced in every atom —
world without end.